WHAT'S IN WORSHIP?

DELIA HALVERSON

CHALICE
PRESS
ST. LOUIS, MISSOURI

Scripture quotations are from the *New Revised Standard Version Bible,* copyright 1989, Division of Christian Education of the National Council of the Churches of Christ in the United States of America. Used by permission. All rights reserved.

Cover image: © Corbis
Cover and interior design: Elizabeth Wright

Visit Chalice Press on the World Wide Web at
www.chalicepress.com

10 9 8 7 6 5 4 3 2 1   09   10   11   12   13

Library of Congress Cataloging-in-Publication Data

Halverson, Delia Touchton.
 What's in worship? / Delia Halverson.
    p. cm.
 ISBN 978-0-8272-4258-6
 1. Worship. I. Title.

 BV10.3.H35 2009
 264—dc22

                                                          2009017286

Printed in United States of America

Contents

Preface

In Genesis we read of Jacob's experience with God when he said, "Surely the LORD is in this place—and I did not know it!" (Gen. 28:16). Sometimes we spend an hour in worship and fail to realize that God is there. Perhaps we have not prepared ourselves for worship or perhaps we have too many other things on our minds. Or perhaps we just don't understand what worship is about. I hope this book will help you discover how God is in your place and time of worship.

I've tried to write this book for the average person who has not been trained in creating a worship experience. I believe it will be helpful for new members of the church and will help parents as they guide their children and youth in understanding just what we do in worship.

Some time back, I chaired a worship committee of a local church. As we discussed worship, I discovered that they knew the various paraments to use on the altar and what colors should be used on what Sundays, but they had no idea whatsoever of the meaning of these worship aids and symbols or of the meaning of any other parts of the service. I wished for such a book as this so that we could have had a study to bring us all to the same understanding of worship. You will find a section in the back of this book that will help you design a study for any group, whether it be a committee of the church or a group of new members.

This book may not include every part of the worship services of your particular church, but it will cover things that are common to most churches. I have not dealt with the newer traditions of the "contemporary" services, because they are many and varied. I have given suggestions in the last chapter of ways to make the liturgical service fresh and exciting.

Delia Halverson
Faith Discovery Ministries
915 Santa Anita Drive
Woodstock, GA 30189

www.deliahalverson.com
halversondelia@bellsouth.net

CHAPTER ONE

What and Why Do We Worship?

Humans have worshiped some idea of God from the beginning of time. Archaeologists continue to find evidence of this as they dig into our past, unearthing cave pictures, altars, objects, and utensils. We see a vast universe out there, and we want to know and understand our connection to it.

Perhaps we are wired with some sort of yearning for our creator, for our connection with that above and beyond us, that which is greater than even our comprehension. A part of that yearning involves an intrigue with the mystery, with the sense of craving for relationship with something so powerful that it goes beyond anything else we encounter. A part of the yearning engages an awe for all that we do not know. And a part of the yearning searches for a personal relationship with what we call God. Mystery, awe, and relationship—all of this leads to worship.

The word *worship* was originally *weorthscripe,* which then became *worthship.* This recognized the importance of God in our lives. In worship, we praise God, learn how desperately we need a relationship with God, and listen to God's direction for using our gifts in service. Worship sets the mode for the rest of life.

We should look at worship as a dialogue. Sometimes we talk to God, and sometimes God talks to us. The worship leaders may speak for us, and they may also speak for God through their words.

Sometimes we worship alone, and sometimes we worship with other people. When we worship in a large group, we usually call this "corporate worship." Jesus said, "For where two or three are gathered in my name, I am there among them" (Mt. 18:20).

Liturgical Worship

In the Christian tradition, forms of what we call liturgical worship evolved over the years. Today many people call this "traditional worship," because we developed specific traditions in this style of worship. "Liturgical worship" has a ritual that keeps us centered and aware. Liturgy can be seen as a rehearsal for life in the world. For this reason we repeat parts of the liturgy over and over. Repetition is a process of making it our own. Many of the rituals of liturgical worship had more meaning to the average person when they were instituted than they do today, but when we learn their original meanings they become alive to us and enhance our modern-day worship.

The word *liturgy* comes from the Greek word *leitourgia*. This means, literally, "public work" or "the work of the people," implying an active role for those of us in the congregation. Liturgy is an imagery for understanding God. If we allow the liturgy to sink into our being, it will change us into living vehicles of God's love.

Worship is an active verb. Rather than a spectator experience or an expectation placed on those up front to entertain us, we should come to worship with an understanding of God as the "audience," we in the congregation as the "actors," and the worship leaders and choir as the "prompters." We come ready to be actively involved. Worship is giving God the glory!

Liturgy also helps us become one with Christians over time. How can we know of God's purpose in the world without learning of those in our past and being with each other? Here we unite, enabled by common prayers. Liturgy forms a bond in community, but must not be exclusive. This has been a problem in the past, and this is why I'm writing this book. When persons do not understand the liturgy, they feel excluded. Christ included everyone. For suggestions on ways to involve newcomers in your worship and church family, see *The Gift of Hospitality*, by Delia Halverson (Chalice Press, 1999).

Personality and Worship

Recent studies have connected our spiritual growth to our personalities. These studies bring a realization that different ways of worship are meaningful to each of us. Our personalities, more than our age, dictate our most meaningful styles of worship.

Some of us are more audio and need a great deal of music in our worship. Others of us are more inclined to the visual, appreciating symbols, pictures, and visual rituals. Some of us are kinesthetic, needing the opportunity to move our bodies as we worship or to see movement in the worship leaders. And some of us worship best in a contemplative and reflective atmosphere, surrounded by silence and perhaps quiet music.

Worship leaders in the past sensed this, even if they had no studies to prove it. They developed liturgical practices that incorporate all of the senses in worship. They had icons, or pictures. They included singing, bells, and musical instruments. They injected times of movement into the service. Sometimes the members of the congregation did the movement, sometimes the worship leader. Worship leaders even involved the sense of smell in their worship, using incense. Anointing with oil and the use of water in baptism involved the sense of feeling. The elements they used to remember the last supper that Christ had with his disciples brought the sense of taste to the worship service.

Sabbath

Most Christians come together to worship on Sunday, although a few continue to celebrate on Saturday. Our Hebrew heritage chose Saturday, the last day of the week, as the "Sabbath." Their specific time for weekly worship is from sundown on Friday to sundown on Saturday. According to the book of Genesis in the Bible, this was the day God rested after creating the world. Early Christians continued to worship with their Hebrew congregations on Saturday, but because Jesus rose from the dead on Sunday, they also came together in their own groups on Sunday. This day was the first day of creation of the universe. As the Christian movement attracted more and more members who were not of the Jewish heritage, they concentrated on their time together on Sunday, so that became their Sabbath. By worshiping on Sunday, we celebrate all that God has done in creating us and the world. We also celebrate the way that God draws us into a personal relationship, through Christ and his death and resurrection. We consider Sundays as "mini-Easters" when we remember the resurrection.

Setting aside a Sabbath time, or a time apart from work each week, is important. It renews the meaning of work and incorporates work with how we involve God in our lives. The observation of a Sabbath time also relates to the release from labor and can be connected with the first Passover and the Hebrews' release from slavery. No matter what the day, a Sabbath gives us a healthy understanding and appreciation of time. It is like a palace in a country of time. The Sabbath can be related to time, as sacred places relate to space. The Sabbath cannot be destroyed as a church building can. Just as we read of the completion of the creation of the world in Genesis, we can see the Sabbath as a day when symbolically all has been accomplished. It is complete, at peace, with a lack of want. Even when we know that Monday will bring the work week back to our lives, we have had a day apart with God and are ready to follow God and experience God's presence in the week ahead.

CHAPTER TWO

Why Worship with Children?

Children are capable of worship, even from their early years. I have seen a small boy stand in awe of some power beyond himself, as he pulled a helium balloon down and then released it again and again. I recall the excitement in my infant grand-daughter's eyes as I carried her into the sanctuary and she looked up at the many lights above her. These children seemed to recognize something beyond their understanding, but something that was at the same time important to them. Children DO worship; they just are not able to express their awe verbally.

Dick Murray was a professor in Christian education at Southern Methodist University. At a pastor's school in South Georgia, he told the story of his three-year-old grandson whom he often took with him in the car. They would sing the Gloria Patri as they traveled through Dallas. He would sit in the front seat singing, "Glory be to the Father...," and his grandson would sit in his car seat in back singing, "Glory Papa; Glory Papa..." One Sunday they were worshiping together and the congregation stood to sing the Gloria Patri. Dick's grandson tugged on his coat and, with shining eyes, he said, "Papa, they're singing our song!"

Dick Murray also said that the first thing a child needs to know is to participate in worship. He felt that every child of school age should know things that are used regularly in worship. This might include the Gloria Patri, the Doxology, and the Lord's Prayer. (see p. 39) Even if they don't understand the words, knowing how to say or sing these things with the congregation helps them feel included and signals the importance of worship.

Why should children be deprived of the opportunity of being involved with their church family in worship? Where else in our society, besides a family reunion, can a child have cross-generation experiences? How can they feel included in the family of the church if they are excluded from the primary purpose of our coming together?

The attention span of children is short; but if they sit close to the front where they can see the activity that is going on, they can become more involved. I recall a family that attended our church for the first time. It just happened that I was at the door when they came in. The father explained that their daughter attended a private Christian school and had asked her parents why they didn't go to a church like her classmates did. I suggested that they be sure to sit close to the front so that their daughter could see what was going on. Several years later the father thanked me for that suggestion. Their daughter had become involved in the church and loved the worship service. She first came to worship as a first or second grader, still of an age when doing what adults do is important.

Why do children belong in worship?
• because they're family
• because we don't ignore family
• because worship is one of the few things that are lasting from childhood to adulthood
• because they learn through experience
• because before third grade they have a window of appreciation for adult actions

Once children pass about the third grade, we lose that window of opportunity where they appreciate adult actions. Soon after that, they find more importance in following their peers than their parents. That is why involving them in corporate worship early is important. Such involvement helps them understand all of the meanings of our worship ritual. After one of the early children's worship studies I conducted, a fourth grader told her mother, "Now I can do what I used to pretend to do!" Although she had worshiped with her parents since she was five years old, all that time she had pretended to understand what was going on, but had not really felt a part of it.

If you wonder why children are inattentive during worship, try sitting at the height of a child's head behind a pew and a row of people. What does the child see? Nothing of interest besides the hymnals and offering envelopes in the pew racks! No wonder these are pulled out of their holders and dropped on the floor. Children find it interesting to get on the floor and look at the different shoes up and down the rows! Sitting in the front pews can make a difference. So can a booster seat for your child so that he or she can see over the pew backs. Perhaps the only difference in a child and adult in worship is that we adults have learned to mask our inattentiveness and a child is truthful about losing attention.

Often children "overhear" something said in a sermon. We may think they are not paying attention because they may be coloring or drawing on the bulletin, but they will key into what is being said, especially if the parents routinely mention positive things about the liturgy or sermon after the service. I recall a four-year-old girl who was coloring in the pew during the sermon. The pastor said, "Now I ask you, where are these people?" The young girl immediately looked up from her coloring and said aloud, "I don't know!"

A worship study for children will help their attentiveness. Encourage your church to develop a worship study that alternates a Sunday of study with a Sunday in the sanctuary with the parent. In this manner they can experience what is being studied. It is hard for a child to apply study to something without experiencing it at the same time.

In appendix 1 you will find some suggestions for parents as they guide their children in a growing appreciation for worship. Parents can also find additional information on helping children grow in understanding of the church in the book, *How Do Our Children Grow?*, by Delia Halverson (Chalice Press, 1999).

Some churches develop young reader's bulletins. These are different from the commercial children's bulletins that you can purchase. The young reader's bulletin follows the same format each Sunday as the adult bulletin, but also contains information about what is happening in the service and provides suggestions and places for children to take notes during specific parts of the service. You will find an example in appendix 3. You can adjust this to your own bulletin format.

If we want our children to appreciate worship when they become adults, we must involve them early and help them understand worship.

CHAPTER THREE

What's in an Order of Worship?

The word *order* is used in many contexts: legal, political, military, science, society, and religious to name a few. Order is generally used in organizing something or labeling parts of an organization. An order of worship then might be defined as a program or plan for a corporate worship service. Churches may use a variety of orders or plans for worship, but most of them follow a basic pattern that goes back to the way Jesus and his disciples worshiped in their synagogues.

Generally the pattern for worship includes four sections:

Entrance: greetings, music, prayer, confession, and praise
Proclamation and Response: scripture, preaching, anthems, hymns, and offering our concerns, prayers, gifts, and service
Thanksgiving and Communion: thanks to God and sharing the bread and cup
Sending Forth: hymn, benediction, or blessing

Christians adapted the first two sections, sometimes called the Service of the Word (preaching), from the ancient synagogue service. Thanksgiving, or the Lord's Supper, commemorates the final meal that Jesus shared with his disciples and reflects the family table worship of the Jewish tradition. Some churches observe the Lord's Supper each Sunday, while some churches do this once a month, once a quarter, and/or on special occasions. We will discuss this further in Chapter 4. The sending forth can be referenced to Jesus' great commission at the end of Matthew:

> And Jesus came and said to them, "All authority in heaven and on earth has been given to me. Go therefore and make disciples of all nations, baptizing them in the name of the Father and of the Son and of the Holy Spirit, and teaching them to obey everything that I have commanded you. And remember, I am with you always, to the end of the age" (Mt. 28:18–20).

Paul's writings reflect some of this pattern, as does Luke's writing (somewhere between 65 and 90 C.E.) in the story of the walk to Emmaus (Lk. 24:13–35).

The two disciples spoke praises of Jesus and poured out their problems, although at the time they did not know that they were speaking with Jesus.	We open our services with greetings, spoken and sung praise, and spoken and sung confessions. We prepare ourselves to receive the Word.
Jesus opened up the scripture, interpreting it for them.	The scripture is read and interpreted through word and music.
The disciples made the decision to respond to Jesus by inviting him to come into their home and have a meal with them.	We respond to the Word by offering our prayers, our gifts, and our dedication to service for the Lord.
Jesus broke bread and shared the cup with them, and then they recognized him.	We celebrate Jesus' life with communion or the Lord's Supper.

Each church develops its own order of worship and may vary it from time to time. The church usually has a bulletin or printed program of some type to help the worshiper follow the action of the service. Here are simple explanations for some of the terms used by many churches in their bulletins.

Welcome and Announcement: We are welcomed and learn of the opportunities for service in our church.

Prelude: We prepare for worship as we listen quietly to the music.

Concerns of the Church: We hear of how we care for our church family.

Ritual of Christian Fellowship: We greet persons near us and record our presence. This time of greeting teaches us to touch each other physically and verbally with love.

Meditation and Silent Confession: We think of things about our life we would like to change and ask God to help us.

Prayer of Confession and Forgiveness: The pastor offers a prayer for our sins and reminds us of our forgiveness. In this prayer we acknowledge our shortfalls, aware of God's love and visioning what we can be.

Affirmation of Forgiveness: The pastor affirms that God forgives us.

Call to Worship: We prepare for worship by reading with the pastor.

Hymn of Praise: We praise God with song. When we sing, the words are given great power if we are aware of their meaning. We share this power with others. Singing hymns of the past connects us with those Christians who followed our faith in the past, and today's songs connect us with Christians around us.

Creed: The creed is a statement of beliefs. Some of the creeds we use were written hundreds of years ago. In the Apostles' Creed, the word *catholic* is not capitalized, showing that it means the universal church and not one specific denomination.

Prayer of Invocation: Our opening prayer, asking God to be with us.

Pastoral Prayer: Prayer for the concerns of the day and people of the congregation.

Our Lord's Prayer: We pray together a prayer that Jesus taught us.

Gloria Patri: We sing a very old song of praise to God.

Children's Message: The pastor has a special time with children.

Morning Prayers: In our prayers, we specially remember persons in need and joys that we have received. We can carry our liturgical prayers into the other days of the week. Praying at set times during each day gives a sacredness to time.

Offertory: We listen to music as we give back to God some of what is given us. These are sometimes called our tithes and offerings. A tithe is a percentage of our income. Biblically we give a tenth of that which comes to us. The liturgical community comes together when we share our gifts. These include our attributes, worldly goods, skills, caring concern, and faith. Paul writes that we are given gifts "to equip the saints for the work of ministry, for building up the body of Christ" (Eph. 4:11–12). Our weekly offerings, skills in worship and other leadership in the church, and our prayers of concern give those gifts back to God.

Doxology: We sing praise to God in response to the gifts given us.

Ministry of Music/Anthem: Sometimes the choir sings, and sometimes we have other music. The music praises God, and sometimes God talks to us through music.

Scripture Lesson: We hear God's word from the Bible. When scripture is read in worship, we can imagine ourselves in what might be called "holy history." We can be transported into the past and then consider how the experience of the past can affect us today.

Message/Sermon: We hear the pastor explain God's word. Through the pastor, God speaks to us and asks us to do certain things.

Invitation to Prayer and Christian Discipleship: The pastor invites us to kneel at the altar to pray and invites persons who want to become a part of the church family to come forward.

Hymn of Invitation: We dedicate ourselves (promise) to do God's work.

Benediction: The pastor sends us out in the world to care. This is not a prayer, but a sending forth. During the benediction, it is appropriate to lift your head to your challenge to take God's word into the world.

Congregational Response: We sing that God's love is in all the world and we will take it to others.

Sometimes the words of a prayer or response may seem strange, especially when the words *Thee* and *Thou* are used. This manner of speaking comes from the Elizabethan Age, when the King James Version of the Bible was translated. At that time the pronouns "thee" and "thou" were only used for family and those personally close to us. "You" and "your" were used for formal situations, including royalty. Today we have completely reversed this usage. When we understand this, we can see God as a very personal deity, not one beyond our reach. This version of the Bible has been used for hundreds of years. Although we have more accurate translations using today's language, many people still love the gentle sounds of the pronouns of that day.

Worship Leaders

Our worship leaders have various responsibilities. The pastors generally take the primary leadership. Sometimes a lay leader will lead part of the worship. This may include the reading of the scripture. Some churches have training classes to train lay leaders to read the scripture with meaning.

The music/choir director may lead the singing. The choir and/or praise team spends many hours rehearsing, not for a performance, but to lead us in worship. Because the special music is not a performance, some churches discourage applause. At times the music seems to move us to some response and the only way we, as worshipers, can often express our joy is through applause. But applause should never be a sign of "good performance." After a contemplative-type anthem, applause may break into our worship attitude and is not appropriate. Just as the words of the hymns express our worship, so the words of the anthem bring us messages from God. It is important to listen closely to these.

Some laypersons act as ushers and greeters. These are more important roles than we may realize. The Old Testament refers to doorkeepers, gatekeepers, and keepers of the threshold. In the New Testament scriptures, Andrew was often called an usher. He brought Peter to Christ (Jn. 1:41–42) and also ushered in the Greek delegation that wished to see Jesus (Jn, 12:20–22). Andrew brought Jesus the young boy who shared his loaves and fishes (Jn. 6:8–9). In the early church ushers not only welcomed persons to worship, but also acted as protectors from the enemies of Christianity. Today ushers not only greet persons and hand out bulletins or programs, but are available for assistance in medical emergencies or if a parent is needed in the nursery. Ushers help when we worship with our tithes and offerings, plus direct us when we come forward to take part in the Lord's Supper. Today ushers may be the first contact a person has upon entering the church building. The gift of hospitality is very important for the usher and the greeter.

Many churches train older children and youths as acolytes. The history of acolytes goes back to the early church when Christians worshiped in the catacombs. The acolyte went ahead of the worshipers, carrying the light into those dark places of worship. Bringing the light into the sanctuary and lighting candles symbolizes Christ as the light of the world. Then, at the close of the service, the acolytes carry the light out, so they remind us that we are to carry the light of Christ into the world. Acolytes may also assist in the dedication of our tithes and offerings and sometimes with a baptism or other acts of worship that the pastors assign.

It is important that the leaders prepare themselves in prayer, asking God to guide them as they assist the congregation in worship. They must recognize that God is the audience and they as leaders are acting as prompters to assist the congregation in acts of worship.

CHAPTER FOUR

What about the Sacraments?

A sacrament may be defined as a "holy moment." The word comes from the Latin word *sacramentum*, which means "an oath of allegiance or an obligation." All Christian churches observe two sacraments, baptism and communion (also called the Eucharist or the Lord's Supper). Some churches, such as the Baptist, prefer not to use the word *sacrament* and call these acts "ordinances." The Roman Catholic Church observes five additional sacraments: confirmation, penance, holy orders, holy matrimony, and anointing of the sick.

Baptism

Although baptism has been observed throughout Christian history, it has been viewed in diverse and even conflicting ways. Although churches may differ in the way that they practice baptism, all Christian churches use the act as an initiation into Christ's church and a means by which we begin our life of following Christ. We are commissioned into the work that God calls us, the work of continuing Christ's redemption of the world. Most churches recognize it as an act of God's divine grace. Some churches insist that persons be baptized in their own denomination even if they have been baptized before, but most churches recognize baptism as a lifelong process by which God works in our lives. Many churches will have services where we can renew our baptismal vows, reminding us of God's grace and of our obligations as followers of Christ.

The use of water in baptism has important symbolism. Water is essential for life. We can go for up to two months without food, but we will die in three days without water. Likewise, Christ is essential for the true life of a Christian. Water cleanses us and also gives us power. Christ cleanses us of our sin, and with Christ we can do all things (Phil. 4:13).

We use several symbols with baptism. The most common symbol is that of a scallop shell with three drops of water below it, reminding us of the Trinity. We also use the dove as we remember that the Gospels tell of a dove coming from heaven at Jesus' baptism (Mt. 3:16; Mk. 1:10; Lk. 3:22). Some churches will use a candle and salt, reminding us of when Jesus told us that we are the salt of the earth and the light of the world (Mt. 5:13–16).

Infant baptism is more than a dedication. In this sacrament God offers the gift of unfailing grace for us to accept for the child. Persons who are baptized as infants have the opportunity to confirm the vows taken by their parents at their baptism. We sometimes call this confirmation. It usually comes after the older child or youth has spent some time studying the Bible and what it means to serve God in whatsoever circumstance he or she finds in life.

Different churches employ one or more of three forms of baptism, and churches differ in whether they baptize infants or have what some churches call "believers' baptism." Some traditions only accept baptism by immersion. This means of baptism not only gives us an image of cleansing and that we are totally immersed in God's love, but also of our death and resurrection through Christ. Some traditions use pouring, where a towel is held under the person being baptized and water is poured from a pitcher or a shell over the head. This gives us an image of God's love being poured out on us. Some traditions use sprinkling, where the water is sprinkled from a bowl or "baptismal font" like rain on the head, reminding us that God's love is spread broadly to all and gives us the spiritual nourishment that we need. Many traditions use all three forms of baptism and will give the person a choice.

In some church buildings, a baptismal font remains at the front of the sanctuary, even when there is no baptism. This is to remind us of our baptismal vows each Sunday. Some churches choose to have the baptismal font at the entrance to the sanctuary so that we can dip our fingers in the water and remember our baptism as we enter and leave worship.

Churches that practice baptism by immersion often have a baptistry at the front of the sanctuary, where the baptismal candidate is immersed in water and rises to new life in Christ in front of the church family. Some congregations will baptize believers in a river or lake.

In some traditions baptism also includes a new name for a new life. When we baptize infants, the name is asked as he or she becomes a part of the Christian community. In any case, we are given a new identity, one in Christ as we become a part of the Christian family. In baptism we recognize our identity. For infants we pledge to "bring up the child" and thereby help the child find his or her own identity.

Communion

Holy Communion may have different names in different traditions. The word *communion* comes from the Latin word for common or a community that has something in common. This term reflects the coming together of the Christian community.

Some churches call the sacrament the Last Supper or the Lord's Supper. The elements we use for this sacrament are symbolic of those used during the last supper that Jesus had with his disciples. The liturgy read during communion usually includes references to that last supper (Mt. 26:17–29; Mk. 14:12–25; Lk. 22:7–20; 1 Cor. 11:23–26). The early church celebrated with what seems to have been a complete meal. In fact, Paul warns the church members about being greedy during the meal (1 Cor. 11:27–34).

This sacrament is also called Eucharist in some churches. This is a Greek word for thanksgiving. We do see this as a time when we are thankful to God for all that we have, especially for sending Christ to us.

As we partake of the communion elements (bread and cup), we symbolically take Christ into our bodies. This acceptance of Christ is as essential to us as our food and drink. The single chalice (cup or goblet) and loaf of bread on the altar/communion table symbolize the unity of Christians.

The elements that we use for communion may vary, even in churches of the same denomination. All churches use some form of bread, representing Christ's body, and drink, representing Christ's blood shed for us. Some churches use a prepared wafer for the bread, and some use broken or cut pieces of bread. During the spoken liturgy, when there is reference to Christ's body being broken for us, the leader usually holds up the bread and sometimes breaks it before us. Many churches now use a type of flat bread that can be torn easily for each person to have a piece. Many churches celebrate the first Sunday in October as World Communion Sunday, when we recognize that persons all over the world are celebrating this sacrament. On that Sunday some churches traditionally use several ethnic breads to remind us of our worldwide Christian family.

The drink is called "the cup" and is also held up when it is referenced in the liturgy. Some churches use wine for the cup, which is probably the drink that was used at the supper that Christ had with his disciples that last night. Water was often impure, so wine was the accepted drink of that day. Today many churches prefer to use grape juice out of respect for persons with addiction problems.

Communion can also be celebrated in several ways. For years most churches served persons individually at an altar rail or in the pew, passing a plate of bread and using small, individual cups. More recently churches use what we call intinction, where we come forward to receive the bread and then partly dip the consecrated bread into the cup. Some churches also follow the tradition of drinking from a common cup.

When the pastor or liturgist indicates that the church practices "open communion," it means that the church accepts anyone to participate who is anxious to follow Christ. In this instance, no affiliation with a particular church is necessary. Some churches practice "closed communion," meaning that only members of that church or of that denomination should partake of communion. This is usually communicated in the worship bulletin or by the priest or minister.

Churches differ in their teachings about what age a person should be to take communion. Even as adults, we don't fully recognize what happens at communion. Realizing this, many churches include young children in communion so that they realize that they are a part of the church family. Other churches want children to be old enough to have been taught certain things before taking communion, and some have a tradition of a "first communion" ritual.

The frequency of celebrating communion will vary with different denominations and churches. Some celebrate it every week, some on the first Sunday of each month. Some churches take the Supper only once a quarter, and other churches celebrate it at special times set aside during the year. Many churches now have a Christmas Eve communion service and most have communion as a part of some service during the week before Easter.

How we celebrate the sacraments is not as important as the fact that we accept the gifts that God gives us during these holy moments. Sacraments are important for us as we worship our God.

CHAPTER FIVE

What Are the Seasons and Symbols?

In medieval times people often believed that visual images, or what they saw, passed through the eye and stamped itself on the soul. There is some truth to this. Today we restrict our children's viewing of the Internet and keep violence and pornography away from them. We need to gather images about us that help remind us of our faith and heritage.

Many books have been written on the Christian seasons and symbols. We can only touch on these seasons and symbols, but perhaps it will help you recognize how such traditions contribute to our worship.

Let's look at the placement of church buildings first. In Europe and early America, church buildings were set in the center of the community not only for convenience, but also to symbolize that all of life revolves around our relationship with God. The church is not on the circumference of our life, but in the center. From it, all life radiates. Many of the buildings have even been shaped in the form of a cross, representing Christ's suffering for us and for the truth that he knew about God. Sanctuaries were also designed in the shape of the cross, with the chancel at the top and two transepts (wings) on either side. It is important to recognize that the church is not the building, but the people who gather and worship there. The building offers a place for the true church, those assembled to serve God, to meet.

Worship Area

The entrance room that leads to the worship area is called the narthex. This room helps us make the transition into a spirit of worship. It reminds us to prepare for worship.

The word *sanctuary* comes from *sanctus*, which literally translated means "holy." Some of the early Christians saw the sanctuary as symbolic of heaven. They saw the dome of the sanctuary as the arching dome of the heavens and painted it with stars. The altar was a symbol of the throne of God. The statues and icons (paintings) of past saints reminded them of the gathering-in of all saints, surrounding God. This helped them feel that they were truly in the presence of God. This is still true in the Orthodox and Roman Catholic traditions.

We speak of the sanctuary as the total worship space, but in the past the sanctuary was the altar and the area behind the altar rail, and the area where the congregation sat was called the nave. The sanctuary, or other designated spaces of worship, gives us a "rooted-ness" that is so lacking in our world today. We have become a nomadic society without roots.

The area at the front of the sanctuary is called the chancel. In some churches this area is raised to signify how we lift God's word above all else in the world. A table placed in the center of the chancel area can signify God as the center of our lives. This is called an altar by some traditions. Others choose not to call it an altar, since Christ's death removed the need to lay sacrifices on an altar. Those traditions call the table a communion table. Whether it is called an altar or a communion table, it can remind us of the plenty of God's table.

Some church buildings have the pulpit at the center of the chancel area, reminding us that the Word of God is central in our lives. This design was popular during the middle of the nineteenth and the early twentieth centuries and is still used in some church buildings today. Some churches use a design that is called a divided chancel. The pulpit, where the preacher delivers the sermon, is on one side. On the other is a lectern, where the liturgist and others assisting in the service stand. Today many preachers choose to move away from the pulpit and speak from the front of the chancel area, believing that this brings the message closer to the people, as well as symbolizes God's word as central in our lives.

Symbols are often built into the architecture, décor, and furniture of our places of worship. In fact, the four-panel door that is also popular in homes was originally designed to remind us of the cross. Explore your building and look for some of these symbols:

Altar/communion table: God is central in our lives. In early church buildings the altar table faced the east, symbolic of receiving the new light, of turning to our beginning and our source of life. This tradition is not as prevalent today as in the past.

Banners: From early times banners have been used in churches. The banners may remind us of specific parts of our Christian life and ministry, or they may remind us of the Christian season or of the many titles for Jesus.

Bible: We use a large Bible to signify the importance of the Bible in our lives. Some churches will bring the large Bible forward in a processional at the beginning of each service, signifying its importance.

Candles/light: Christ as the light of the world. We often use two candles to remind us that Jesus was both human and divine.

Chalice: Cup for communion. Christ's blood shed for us.

Circle: God's eternal and everlasting love.

Cross: Christ's death for our salvation.

Empty cross: Christ's resurrection.

Flowers: In the sanctuary fresh flowers remind us of the living Christ who rose from the dead to give us new life.

Grapes: Christ's blood.

High ceilings: Symbolizing our reaching upward to God.

Paraments: The cloths used on the altar and pulpits, and as stoles.

Robes: One of the robes worn by worship leaders came from the uniform of scholars in medieval universities. The robe with a hood, or alb (Latin for "white"), was part of the everyday dress worn by Roman men and women prior to 400 C.E. (that is, the Christian Era, the same as A.D.)

Square: Four gospels of Matthew, Mark, Luke, and John.

Stained-glass windows: These were first used when the common people could not read. The stories in the windows helped them remember the Bible.

Triangle/3 circles: Trinity—the three ways we relate to God are as creator/parent, Jesus in human form, and Holy Spirit within us.

Wheat: Bread of life; Christ's body as broken bread

Seasons of the Christian Year

Christian churches use the cycle of seasons to bring before us, each year, the life of Jesus and its impact on the world. In the early days of Christendom, the resurrection of Christ was the only special day celebrated. It held the prime impact of Jesus' life on Christians, as well as promise of the future. Churches still celebrated the Jewish holy days. As the years went on, the church dropped the Jewish holy days and added more and more

Christian celebrations. The yearlong cycle leads from one to the next, so we see the whole of Jesus' life and his challenge to us to go into the world throughout the year.

Advent

Advent is the first season of the cycle, though it was not the first one celebrated by the early church. We celebrate Advent the four Sundays before Christmas. It is a time of anticipation and preparation. The word *advent* comes from the Latin word *adventus,* which means "arrival" or "coming."

The color purple is a royal color because of the time and expense required to produce purple dye. It took thousands of the body parts of tiny Murex shells to produce a few drops of purple dye. Purple helps us recognize Christ as our king. We also use blue during Advent. It is considered Mary's color and represents hope. Some of the symbols we use include the wreath (representing God's eternal love), evergreens (the ever-living God), candles (Christ as the light of the world), trumpets (prophecy), poinsettia and rose (blood Christ shed for us), and bells (declaring the joy of Christ's coming).

Christmas

Christmas begins on Christmas Eve and lasts for twelve days until Epiphany. It is the celebration of Christ's birth. We actually have no exact knowledge of the time of Jesus' birth. However, it is appropriate that Christians of the fourth century established the date of celebration near the winter solstice. At that time the days begin to lengthen and more light comes into the world. We recognize Christ as the light, or dayspring, of the world.

The color for Christmas is white, signifying purity and light. We use many of the same symbols as Advent. Some churches do not add the Christ Child to nativity sets until Christmas Eve.

Epiphany

Epiphany is celebrated on January 6. The word *epiphany* means "to go forth." The magi set out on their epiphany, searching for the Christ Child. When they left on their return journey, they went forth, spreading the good news to other countries.

The color for Epiphany is green, representing growth. We remember how Christ's message was spread by the magi. We do not actually know the number of magi who came to see Jesus, but three gifts are mentioned in Matthew. Some of the symbols we use include crowns (royalty), gifts (the gifts of gold, frankincense, and myrrh), and star (led the magi).

Season after Epiphany

Season after Epiphany extends from Epiphany to Ash Wednesday. This is an "Ordinary Season." The use of the word *ordinary* does not mean commonplace or plain, but comes from the Latin word *ordinal,* which means "time in order." The season after Epiphany is anything but plain and simple. It emphasizes the life and teachings of Jesus. This time helps us move from the childhood of Jesus through his ministry. During this season we get into the heart of Jesus' message. It prepares us to live the life of a true follower of Christ.

The color for this season is also green, a color for growth, indicating our growth as a Christian. To symbolize the growth theme of this season, we use the symbol of a sprouting plant. We also use symbols from Jesus' life such as a fish or fishnet (symbolizing times that Jesus spoke of fishing, such as Matthew 4:19) or water, shells, and the dove (symbolizing his baptism as told in Mt. 3:13–17, Mk. 1:9–11, and Lk. 3:21-22). We may also use symbols from the parables Jesus told, such as stones, seeds, pearls, coins, and sheep. Some churches center on the great "I am" statements from Jesus, using symbols of bread (Jn. 6:35), light (Jn. 8:12), gate (Jn. 10:7–9), shepherd (Jn. 10:11–16), vine

(Jn. 15:1), and way/road (Jn. 14:6). We remember that "I am" is the name that God told Moses to use for God (Ex. 3:1–14).

Lent

Lent is a forty-day period before Easter beginning on Ash Wednesday. In counting those forty days we do not include Sundays which are considered "mini-Easters." In some churches Lent is a time of fasting, and since Sunday was a "feast day," it could not be included in the days of Lent. The use of the number forty is popular in the Bible and is a number representing fullness, or the amount of time it took for something to be accomplished. Lent is a time we prepare for Easter, reflecting on our spiritual growth. We use purple during Lent, a color for penitence, reflection, and the royalty of Christ.

The cross is the primary symbol used during Lent. The cross can remind us that we divide the world into the four directions of north, south, east, and west. We stand with Christ at the center of those four directions, at the center of the world so to speak. Christianity is inclusive of all in the world, not exclusive. More than fifty styles of crosses are found in Christian art, but the most common one is the Latin cross which the Romans used to execute criminals. This symbol of death is appropriately transformed into a symbol of life for Christians.

Holy Week is the last week of Lent, recalling Jesus' last week before his crucifixion. On Palm (or Passion) Sunday, the Sunday before Easter, we remember when Jesus rode into Jerusalem on a donkey (Mt. 21:1–11; Mk. 11:1–11; Lk. 19:28–44; Jn. 12:12–19). Jesus rode a donkey as a sign of peace. When kings came in war to conquer a city, they rode on a horse, but when they came in peace they rode an ass or donkey. These actions move us to call Christ the King of Peace. People placed branches in his path, and since palms are common in Jerusalem, we use palm branches to symbolize this event.

The color black on Good Friday reminds us of the darkness we have without Christ. The word *passion* comes from a Latin word that means "to suffer." During Holy Week we also celebrate the last meal that Jesus had with his disciples (Lk. 22:7–38). The symbols for communion are used here, as well as a pitcher and towel (Jn. 13:1–17). Good Friday is the dark time of Holy Week. For this day we usually drape the cross in black. A large hammer and three spikes are also used to symbolize this day. Other events of Holy Week can be symbolized with coins (Mt. 26:14–16), whip (Mt. 27:26), crown of thorns (Mark 15:17), and a rooster (Mt. 26:74–75).

Easter

Easter begins on Easter Sunday and lasts for fifty days until Pentecost. This is when we celebrate the resurrection of Christ. The exact origin of the word *Easter* is uncertain. It may have been adapted from another spring celebration. This practice was common in the past. The early Jewish Christians celebrated the resurrection of Christ three days after Passover, which could cause it to happen any day of the week. However, the Gentile Christians insisted that it be celebrated on Sunday. In 325 C.E., the church set the date to celebrate Easter as the first Sunday after the full moon crosses the spring equinox. Because the equinox changes from year to year, Easter may come in either March or April, varying as much as thirty-five days.

We use white and gold for the Easter season. White symbolizes purity and the newness of victory over sin and death. Gold (or yellow) reminds us of Christ as the king who came to enlighten the world. Some churches will release butterflies on Easter Sunday. (See www.insectlore.com and www.butterflywebsite.com.) The cycle of a butterfly reminds us of Jesus' time in the tomb and how he came from the tomb to give us new life. The bulb of a lily appears to be dead until it is put in the ground.

Then it comes to life, reminding us of Christ's resurrection. Other flowers and baby animals can also remind us that Christ brought us new life. The peacock that sheds and re-grows its feathers and the phoenix, the mythical bird that rose from ashes, are sometimes used as symbols of Easter.

Pentecost

Pentecost is the fiftieth day (seventh Sunday) after Easter. It is sometimes called the birthday of the church. The word comes from the Greek word *pentekoste* meaning the fiftieth [day]. This was actually a day of Hebrew celebration called the Day of First Fruits (Num. 28:26). It was also called the Festival of Weeks or Shabuoth (Ex. 34:22; Num. 28:26; Deut. 16:10, 16; 2 Chr. 8:13; Tob. 2:1; 2 Mac. 12:31) or the feast of harvest (Ex. 23:16). The disciples were gathered in a closed room, not yet ready to face the world with Christ's message. We read how the Holy Spirit came as a rushing wind and flames of fire (Acts 2:1–42). The disciples were not only given courage to begin their ministry but were also given an ability to speak in various languages, so that the many visitors to Jerusalem were able to understand their message.

We use red, the color of flames, for Pentecost. Some of the symbols we use represent the Holy Spirit. Tongues of flames, doves, kites, pinwheels, and curling lines remind us of the rush of wind that blew through the room. Some churches have even used red-hot peppers to represent how the early Christians were on fire for Christ.

Season after Pentecost

Season after Pentecost is sometimes called "Ordinary Season." It lasts from the Sunday after Pentecost until Advent begins. During this season we emphasize spreading the gospel and missions. The Sunday after Pentecost is called Trinity Sunday; the

Sunday before Advent begins is called Christ the King Sunday. It is important during this season that we work with peace, forgiveness, and community building in our own churches and the community around the world. Churches also emphasize the way that we are co-creators with God and stewards of the earth.

Some churches will continue to use red during the first weeks of the Season after Pentecost, while some will immediately switch to green. In this case, the color green reminds us of how Christianity has grown around the world and how we must be involved in continuing to nurture that growth, spreading Christ's message and ministry. Some symbols we might use during this season include potter's wheel or pottery (we are vessels to carry God's message), oxen yoke (we accomplish God's work when yoked with Christ), loom or woven fabric (God's message is for all peoples), and broken wall (Christ's message breaks barriers).

And so we make it around the cycle of the year. When we understand the Christian seasons, we learn to follow the events of God's grace and make them a part of our present life. As you see, the seasons and all of these symbols can easily be used to teach us about Christ, the life he lived, and the message he brought to us. We best learn through our senses, which even the early church realized as it set up traditions and customs using all five senses.

For more information and suggestions about the Christian seasons, see *Teaching and Celebrating the Christian Seasons* (Chalice Press, 2002) and *Children's Activities for the Christian Year* (Abingdon Press, 2004), both by Delia Halverson.

Other Special Days

All Saints' Day is the bright side of what we now know as Halloween. Many Christians see Halloween as the dark side of a holiday, symbolizing life without Christ. All Saints' Day on November 1, on the other hand, symbolizes those persons who lived in the past and those living today who follow Christ. Most Protestant churches consider all those who follow Christ as saints rather than only those determined so by an official church body.

Ascension Day is celebrated on the fortieth day of Easter, remembering the day that Christ ascended to heaven. Since it is forty days after Easter Sunday, it always occurs on Thursday. This day was celebrated more widely in early Christendom.

Bible Presentation to middle elementary children has become a special day in many churches. It is important that some training in the reading of the Bible accompany this presentation. In some churches, the Bible is presented to the parent(s) first. The parent(s) then presents it to the child, because the parent has responsibility, with the help of the church, for sharing faith with the child.

Confirmation has become a special day in many Protestant churches. This is a time when persons who have made a study of what it means to be a Christian and who now confirm the vows taken by/for them at their baptism are recognized as full members of the church. It is not a graduation, but rather a beginning of a life dedicated to Christ and a life of study to follow God's calling in every way.

Reformation Sunday commemorates October 31, 1517, when Martin Luther posted his statements on the church doors, an action which began the Protestant Reformation.

Thanksgiving is a time of worship as well as celebration. Our biblical roots extend to Old Testament days when Hebrews celebrated three feasts of thanksgiving: Passover for the barley harvest (release from slavery in Egypt), Pentecost (feast of first fruits or weeks) for the wheat harvest, and Feast of Tabernacles or Booths for grapes and olives (also called Sukkoth or ingathering), an eight-day, end of fall harvest festival. Symbols of things for which we are thankful are appropriate at this time. Some churches borrow from their Hebrew heritage and create a sukkah, a booth or three-walled open shed, with fruits and vegetables hung from overhead poles. The Hebrew sukkah symbolized Israel's life in the wilderness and later came to represent the "temporariness" of life on earth (Lev. 23:40-43).

Trinity Sunday, the Sunday after Pentecost, is the time when we recognize the way that we celebrate God in three persons: God revealed to us as our creator or parent, in human form through Jesus (God with "skin on"), and as the Holy Spirit (God within us). Symbols that we use for Trinity Sunday may include three intertwined circles, a triangle, trefoil, shamrock, or fleur-de-lis.

World Communion is a time we celebrate the unity of Christ throughout the world. Christians around the globe celebrate communion on the first Sunday in October as we recognize our unity in Christ. We reflect on our role in the community around us as well as throughout the world.

CHAPTER SIX

What's in a Hymnal?

Some might think that hymnals are a thing of the past, with so many churches turning to projection of words on the screen. But hymnals have a real place in today's worship. The psalmist said, "Sing to him a new song; Play skillfully on the strings, with loud shouts" (Ps. 33:3)." One of our major hymn writers of the past was Charles Wesley. Many of his songs used popular pub tunes of the day that most people knew. His brother John instructed those in the Methodist movement to "sing lustily and with good courage." To sing lustily, we must first learn the hymns, and persons who can read music can learn the hymns much easier with the notes before them.

Other reasons encourage us to appreciate the hymnal. Between the covers is a wealth of great material. First to consider are the words of the hymns, then we look at creeds that can be found in most hymnals. Finally, we investigate the other worship aids that many hymnals contain.

Hymns

Even if we never sang a note of music, we could use the words of the hymns to draw us closer to God. We can use hymns for study, to initiate thoughts, and even to form our prayers. Some hymns may seem to have a burden of verses, but the words of the verses tell a story or offer a prayer and the refrain accents the theme.

The words in the hymns are filled with symbolism. Among other images, Christ is called King, Emmanuel, Wisdom, Root of Jesse's tree, Dayspring, Desire, Word of God, Shepherd, Lamb, Mother, Father, and Rock of Ages. You will find that you can connect with some of the images mentioned in the hymns, while others seem foreign. But know that our hymns are written for a wide variety of people, so they each mean something special to different people.

Your hymnal will probably have a variety of ancient songs of praise that have been sung down through the ages. The psalms were the hymns of Jesus' day, and we still use many of them today. Many churches use the Gloria Patri, which was sung as early as the fourth century. The name is Latin for "Glory be to the Father." The hymnal also offers doxologies, or short hymns of praise. A popular one, "Praise God from Whom All Blessings Flow," was written as the thirteenth stanza of a hymn in 1674.

Most hymnals have several indexes in the back. These may include the following areas:

Index of first lines and common titles	If you remember the first line or a title of a hymn, this index will help you locate it.
Index of topics and categories	When you are looking for a hymn on a particular subject, this index is very helpful. Besides the Christian seasons and aspects of Jesus' life, you will find subjects such as adoration and praise, calmness and serenity, children, faith, grief, hope, love, prayer, and trust.

Index of scripture	Many of our hymns use words or themes from scripture, such as "O God, Our Help in Ages Past" (Psalm 90). Using the words of the hymns helps us better understand the scripture.
Index of composers, authors, and sources	Although this index may be used primarily by those selecting and preparing music, it is interesting to look at the persons of our Christian heritage who contributed to our worship. You may find that some of those listed contributed as many as fifty hymns. Some of the hymns come from different ethnic backgrounds.
Index of tune names	Unless we are musicians, most of us do not know the tune names. But you will see from this index that the words of several hymns can be used with the same tunes.
Metrical index	This index helps a musician know which tunes are compatible, and alternate tunes may be used if the musician feels a tune is too difficult or unfamiliar.

Our hymnals certainly aid us in worship. It would do every Christian well to get to know the contents and use it in any way to help him or her grow in the faith. The hymnal provides a wealth of Christian witness from throughout the life of the church.

Creeds or Affirmations of Faith

A creed or an affirmation of faith is a list or statement of beliefs. Through the years many persons and communities of faith have formed creeds to express their understanding of the Christian faith. We use creeds from our heritage and creeds from today. The basic beliefs that are in most of our creeds include belief in God expressed in four ways: in forgiveness of our sins, in the communion or fellowship of Christians, in the resurrection of the body and life everlasting, and in the universal church.

Sometimes creeds have special words or phrases in them that are used primarily in Christianity. When we speak of God's grace, we mean an unconditional love or an "I love you anyway" type love. If a creed or other liturgy says "holy unto God," this indicates specialness, even without one doing anything to warrant it. If the creed uses a small "c" for the word *catholic,* it means the universal church, not a particular church tradition.

You may find creeds or affirmations of faith in the hymnal using words from scripture. Here are passages that are often used for creeds:

Romans 8:35, 37–39
1 Corinthians 15:1–6
Colossians 1:15–20
1 Timothy 1:15; 2:5–6; 3:16

The Nicene Creed is recited in many Christian churches. Its original form was adopted by the first ecumenical council, meeting in Nicaea in 325 C.E. Another of the oldest creeds of the Christian church, the Apostles' Creed, was written almost 2,000 years ago. Many churches use one of these ancient creeds from time to time, while some churches use one every week. The language may not be such as we would write today, but it connects us with many persons who have professed our faith throughout the years. If for no other reason than this, it is important for us to use a creed at times. It connects us with our Christian heritage down through the ages.

You may find other creeds in your hymnal. Recently various ethnic groups have developed their own creeds, using some of their cultural language. Some churches even encourage confirmation classes to create their own creeds as they study what it means to be a Christian.

Other Worship Aids

In your hymnal you will probably find several other worship aids. Almost every hymnal has a written copy of the Lord's Prayer. This prayer is universal throughout the Christian church. The prayer comes from Matthew 6:9–13. There is a shorter version in Luke 11:2–4. The last phrase concerning God's kingdom, power, and glory in Matthew's account comes from 1 Chronicles 29:10–13. Here is a simple explanation of the words of this prayer, first printed in *Teaching Prayer in the Classroom* (Abingdon Press, 1989) 27–28, (rev. ed. 2003) 55–56.

Our Father,	Because God is like a good *father*, Jesus used the word *Father*. By using the word *our* we realize that God loves all of us and wants us to work together.
who art in heaven,	The word *art* is an old way of saying "are." When we speak of God being in heaven, it does not mean far away, but rather that God is everywhere and greater than we can understand.
Hallowed be thy name.	*Hallowed* is a way of praising God, another word for holy, awe, or wonder.
Thy kingdom come, Thy will be done, on earth as it is in heaven.	With these words we pray that all of us on earth will live as God wants, loving each other.
Give us this day our daily bread,	When we pray for "our daily bread," we realize that God made the world that produces food for us to eat. Food is also a part of God's plan, and God is a dependable God. We also realize that all our daily needs are important to God. Notice that Jesus did not use *my* daily bread, but *our*. The prayer doesn't ask for everything we want each day, but for what we need.

And forgive us our debts,	We recognize that we all sin. The word *debt* is a very old word for sin. Sometimes when we pray we use the word *trespass*, which in this context is another word for sin. The real meaning for sin is that we "separate ourselves from God." When we sin, we do something or think something that keeps us from being close to God. We ask God to forgive us, knowing that we are forgiven if we are truly sorry.
As we forgive our debtors	We also tell God that we forgive others of sins against us. We realize that we must forgive in order to set ourselves right with God.
And lead us not into temptation. But deliver us from evil.	A temptation is when we want to do something other than what God wants us to do. We realize that God's help is available for us and know that we will need to follow God's good plan for us.

In most versions of the Bible, this is where Matthew's direct quotation from Jesus ends. However, as early as the third century people were using this prayer in their worship services, and they found such joy over the words of the prayer that they just continued the prayer, using some of the words from 1 Chronicles 29:10¬13 *(King James Version)*. The following words have been added by tradition and are commonly used with the passage from Matthew.

For thine is the kingdom, and the power, and the glory,	The close of the prayer again says that we believe that God is over all the world and universe (kingdom) and is the greatest.
Forever!	We know that God is forever, with no end.
AMEN.	The word *amen* means "I agree," or "May it be so."

One section of the hymnal may have responsive readings. If a section is labeled a Psalter, it contains biblical psalms. In these readings the leader reads a part, then the congregation responds with a sentence or two. Usually the leader's reading is printed in regular print and the congregation's response is in bold print. This style of worship reflects our Hebrew heritage, where the priest or cantor read or sang and the people responded. Sometimes we will even sing the words back and forth. Singing in this manner is referred to as antiphonal singing. When we read or sing responsively, we become more involved in worship. This helps us leave our spectator position and personally enter into worship.

Many of the responsive readings are drawn from scripture, particularly the book of Psalms. This is a marvelous book in the Bible with expressions that easily reflect situations today. The writers, or psalmists, used expressions of joy and praise, but they also expressed their feelings of frustration and anger. As we read them, we recognize that God is great enough to be able to withstand our anger, so we can express that anger to God and still receive the unqualified love that we call grace.

Besides the Lord's Prayer and Psalter, you may find some of the following aids to worship:

- Services of Baptism
- Services of Communion or the Lord's Supper (or Word and Table)
- Service of Christian Marriage
- Service for the Dead

Your church may also have another book with worship aids from which the pastor draws for other special services. The book may include church membership or confirmation, special dedications, commissioning and ordinations, blessings, love feast or agape meal, thanksgiving of birth or adoption of a child, presentation of Bibles, recognition of volunteers, and healing services.

CHAPTER SEVEN

How Is a Liturgical Worship Service Designed?

I have used computers since 1981 and feel quite comfortable with them. However, I recently became a coach for senior adults in my community who are learning to use computers. Some students never touch the machine from one week to the next. Others either work with the lesson at home or find a computer where they can practice. The ones who spend time working with the computer between sessions are the ones who really learn how to use it. This experience reinforced what I knew about learning. We can read all we can find about something, but in reality the learning is in the doing.

You will understand more about worship and will gain much more from your participation in a worship service if you work with designing one. In this chapter you will learn just how worship leaders design a service, and you can use the format to design one of your own. You may want to check with your pastor about designing a service that can actually be used for worship in your church.

Use the form in appendix 2 to help design your worship service, or simply create your own. Decide on a theme, select a scripture, and use the indexes in your hymnal to find hymns and other resources. Go back to the descriptions on pages 12–14 as you develop your service. If it is a seasonal service, review the section on that particular season. You may find additional resources in your church library.

Although a liturgical worship service generally follows a specific order, no rules demand that it do so. You have many opportunities and resources to make the service fresh and exciting. Here are some suggestions that you might include to make your service unique:

- Have the lights dimmed when persons enter. When the first hymn begins, turn on all lights. Place a statement like this in the bulletin: "We enter a dimly lit sanctuary and then turn on the lights to remind us that Christ, whom we worship, is sometimes called the 'dayspring' of life," or "We enter a dimly lit sanctuary and then during the first hymn turn on the lights to remind us that Christ, whom we worship, is the light of the world."

- Create a visual imagery to emphasize the scripture. Here are some ideas you might use:

  Genesis 1:27–31 (a variety of seeds)
  Genesis 2:4–10 (a clear bowl with water, or a fountain, and a pile of dirt)
  Joshua 4:1–9 (twelve rocks stacked together)
  Psalm 23 (sheepskin and shepherd's crook)
  Psalm 92:1–5 (musical instruments)
  Psalm 119:105 (lamp and Bible)
  Proverbs 12:12 (a clean root)
  Isaiah 40:28–31 (running shoes)
  Jeremiah 18:1–4 (potter's wheel or a collection of pottery and broken pieces)
  Matthew 5:15 (a candle with a bushel basket propped above)

Matthew 7:24–27 (large rock)

Matthew 11:28–30 (a yoke and a candle representing Christ)

Luke 21:1–4 (large stack of money on one side and a few coins on other)

John 21:1-14 (breakfast of grilled fish and bread, with fishnet)

Hebrews 12:1–2 (victory flag)

- Include a strolling actor in your worship to tell the scripture story in costume. You might use these scriptures, giving viewpoints from the following.

Genesis 5:28–9:28 (Noah)

Exodus 3:1–17 (Moses at the burning bush)

Joshua 3:1–4:9 (one of the men appointed to place a rock)

Isaiah 9:2–7 (Prophet Isaiah giving the scripture reading)

Luke 1:26–56 (Elizabeth)

Luke 2:1–20 (Mary, Joseph, or the innkeeper)

Matthew 2:1–12 (Mary, Joseph, or one of the magi)

Luke 2:41–52 (Mary, Joseph, or a relative of the boy Jesus)

Luke 4:16–30 (a neighbor of Jesus)

Mark 1:40–45 (the leper)

Mark 2:23–28 (one of the disciples)

John 6:1–15 (the disciple Andrew or the young boy grown up)

John 13:1–17 (Peter who didn't want his feet washed)

Mark 15:22–47 (one of the soldiers)

John 20:1–18 (Mary Magdalene)

Acts 2:1–13 (a visitor from another country at Pentecost)

This list includes only a few of many stories that can be applied in this manner. Any event can be told by someone on the scene or any of Jesus' parables can be told by a listener or one of the disciples. The healing miracles can be told by the one receiving the healing. Use your imagination.

- Remember that in the sermon the preacher speaks for, from, by, and to: *for* God, *from* the scriptures, *by* the authority of the church, and *to* the people. As the preacher prepares the sermon, he/she tries to help us answer these questions: How do the words of the sermon make the scripture relate to my life? What will happen to my life because of this sermon? What is the scripture saying to me specifically?

- Use readings and hymn times to explain decorations of the sanctuary for specific occasions, such as the greenery for Advent and flowers on an empty cross for Easter. (For a "Hanging of the Greens" Sunday morning service, see appendix 3 in *Teaching and Celebrating the Christian Seasons* by Delia Halverson (Chalice Press, 2002).

- Use "heritage bells" as a way of remembering people in our past on special occasions. Give each person a bell as they enter. Ask them to pin the bell on a streamer in memory or honor of someone who has helped them grow in their faith. Then at one or more points in the service, have someone move the streamers to ring the bells.

- Ask each family to bring a small glass from home to use during a communion service. This glass is then taken home as a remembrance of the service. Have extras available for those who are unaware of the request.

- Begin a service outside, then move into the sanctuary with the first hymn. For Epiphany you can have magi in costume to come out of the crowd and ask, "Have you seen the child that was supposed to be born?" The leader answers, "Will you come with me?" and then leads the magi and the congregation into the sanctuary. For Easter give everyone candles or flowers to take into the sanctuary, remembering how the women rose early and went to the tomb. Once inside, flood the room with light and decorate with the flowers.

- Use a guided imagery journey in the service. The leader will be the guide. For the story of Jesus plucking the grain (Mt. 12:1–8), begin something like this, "We are walking along the road with Jesus and come to a wheat field. It's afternoon and you've had nothing to eat since early morning. Several of the disciples walk into the field and begin eating the grains, so you follow them. Suddenly a Pharisee from the back of the crowd rushes up to Jesus."

- Have someone do some action in the chancel area to the side during the singing of a hymn or reading of the scripture or during the entire service. This might be weaving when the service is about our Christian heritage or diversity; painting a picture to illustrate a point; folding baby clothes for Advent; cutting up dead Christmas trees to form a cross for Lent; making a crown of thorns; or making a kite for Pentecost. Place a statement in the bulletin that explains the meaning behind the action.

- Have persons stand as statues from a scene in the story as the scripture is read. They don't even need to be in costume.

- Use a mime or sign language during the reading of the scripture.

- During a greeting time, ask everyone to use a specific sentence, such as "You are a gift from God" or "Christ has risen!" This might be done in another language on Pentecost, World Communion Sunday, or some other occasion.

- Use a quiet time for centering during the service, asking persons to listen for the Holy Spirit in their lives.

- At Advent or at Pentecost, use a birthday cake with twelve candles, and at one point during the service light a candle for each month, asking everyone with birthdays during that month to bring a mission offering forward.

- Invite the congregation to spontaneously express their beliefs in a creed. Ahead of time ask two people for each of the three sections to be prepared to offer a word or phrase in their respective areas. To do this, print the following in the bulletin:

We believe that God comes to us in many ways.
We believe that God created these things:
> *(During this time, feel free to mention aloud things that you recognize as created by God.)*

We believe that God came in human form, and through Jesus taught us these things:
> *(During this time, feel free to mention out loud various truths that Jesus taught.)*

We believe that God works within us as the Holy Spirit:
> *(During this time, feel free to mention out loud ways that the Holy Spirit helps us live better lives.)*[1]

- At a point in the service, ask each person to draw or write on a 3x5 card something he or she can offer of self to someone else. Then either have them place those cards in the offering or bring them to the front.

---

[1]Delia Halverson, *Teaching and Celebrating the Christian Seasons* (St. Louis: Chalice Press 2002), 80.

APPENDIX 1

Parents and Children
Worship Together[1]

As you worship together as a family, your attitude toward worship will signal its importance. Worship is a celebration of God's love. Our response to worship is an acting out of God's love. These two are coupled, and one is incomplete without the other.

God initiates our relationship and calls us to become an inclusive family. Worship, in some ways, is like a family meal. Individuals in a family can, and sometimes do, eat separately. But there is a deeper enjoyment in a meal when we share it with other members of the family.

We worship independently at times. It is important to be able to worship spontaneously at any place, alone. However, if we never worship as a church family, with all of the church family, then we miss the depth of love that can grow between worshipers.

Get to know the place of worship better. Visit the sanctuary when it is empty. Walk around from place to place. Talk about what happens during the service. Look at the items in the pew rack and explain them to your child. Explain the communion cup holders fastened to the pew. Open a hymnal and show him or her how you follow the words of a hymn, one verse at a time.

---

[1]Part of the material for this appendix comes from Delia Halverson, *How Do Our Children Grow?* (St. Louis: Chalice Press, 1999), 98–103.

Decide on a place you will want to sit. Children can usually see better up close. Sometimes an additional cushion or booster seat will help the child see better.

Talk about and get to know the leaders of worship. Your child probably knows some of them, but introduce him or her to others such as ushers and even members of the worship committee.

Practice the responses and prayers frequently used in the service. Your child may have been praying the Lord's Prayer in the past, but spend some time actually reading it and talking about it. Sometimes when the prayer is learned by rote, words are mistaken. This can cause embarrassment for children. Pray the Lord's Prayer (see p. 39) at bedtime or in the morning. From time to time, use the Doxology for the blessing before meals.

Practice whispering and explain to your child that he or she can ask you questions about the worship service on Sunday, but that in order not to disturb others, you will whisper.

Decide on persons you want to pray for as a family. Explain that during one of the prayers the pastor mentions special people we want to pray for, you can tell God silently in your heart the ones you specially want to pray for.

On Saturday night see that your child is in bed early. It is as important to be rested for the Sunday worship as it is for school on Monday. Make a rule of no overnights on Saturday, unless they agree to early bedtime and attending church with you the next morning. Decide on clothing and lay it out.

On Sunday morning plan ample time to eat a good breakfast and prepare for church. A child with a hungry stomach is naturally restless. If your child avoids certain foods or uses a medication on school days, follow the same procedure for Sundays. Before you wake your child, tune the radio to a Christian station or turn on a tape of religious music to set the mood. You'll be surprised how it helps you too! Allow plenty of travel time so that you aren't rushed.

When you arrive at church, be certain that your child has made use of the restroom and will not need to go during the service. If your child can go an hour and a half between restroom breaks at school, it's also possible at church.

Use the time after you take your seats to locate hymns and responses, using bookmarks, and mark things in the bulletin that you will be doing during the week. Then say, "I need to be quiet and talk with God before the service and so do you. Ask God to help the minister and the choir. Ask God to help us worship."

Tools to Help During Worship:

1. File cards to hold under the line of hymns and move from line to line.

2. Bookmarks prepared ahead and used to mark places in the hymnal and pew Bible as you wait for the service to begin. If you use red, white, and blue for the first, second, and third item, your child will know the order.

3. Package of fine-line magic markers to use with the bulletin. Use different colors to mark times we pray, we sing, we listen to music, we hear God's word, etc. These are action words which help your child recognize that doing these actions is taking part in worship.

4. Pencil and paper or note cards to use for note taking. Encourage your child to make a note or draw a picture as a reminder of something specific to discuss with you after the service. Feel free to take notes yourself, so your child develops the practice of listening for specific things in the sermon to talk about later.

5. Money for the child's offering should be decided on before the service. If your child receives an allowance, help him or

her decide on a specific amount of the allowance that will be the child's contribution to church. Always include the child in the offering part of worship.

6. Arms are for hugging. They are the best tools you can use during the service to encourage your child. Tell him or her how happy you are to be worshiping together. Let your child lean against you, have physical contact, ask you questions, and have your attention. Remember that you are helping to form your child's relationship with God, and no one can do it better than you.

Seasonal colors and symbols are a way of helping us remember and understand. Explain some of these to your child.

- **Purple:** This color of royalty is used during Advent and Lent.
- **Blue:** Symbol of hope, it sometimes is used during Advent.
- White: Purity's color is displayed at Christmas, Easter, and for communion.
- **Green:** The color of growth predominates at Epiphany and the seasons after Epiphany and after Pentecost.
- **Red:** Flame's color is used at Pentecost and sometimes the season after Pentecost.
- **Circles:** God's love is everlasting.
- **Arches:** God is over and all around us.
- **Triangles:** The experience of God as Trinity comes in three ways: parent, human form (Jesus), Holy Spirit (within us)
- **Squares:** The four gospels are Matthew, Mark, Luke, John.
- **Fish:** In this early symbol of church, we "fish" for persons by sharing God's love. The Greek term for fish is *Ixthus.* These letters represent for us who Jesus is: I (*Iesous,* Jesus); X (*Xristos,* Christ); Th (*Theos,* God); U (*uios,* son), S (*soter,* Savior).

Permission is granted to photocopy these pages for congregational use.

- **Light/candles:** We bring light into sanctuary to remind us that God is with us. Taking it out reminds us that we take God into the world.
- **Bread and cup:** Communion is the reminder of the last meal Jesus had with his disciples and what he did in letting his body be broken and his blood spilled.
- **Grapes and wheat:** These are sources of the communion elements.
- **Stained glass:** Pictures were used in church buildings to tell Bible stories when people could not read the Bible.
- **Shell and water:** Baptism washes us clean with God's love.
- **Offering plates:** We give back some of what God has given us.

After the service, talk about positive things that happened during the morning. Make honest, positive comments about what worship meant to you. Decide what changes should be made in your own life because of the service, so your child learns to apply the worship service to his or her own life. Listen to your child's comments. Remember that we can often learn from children. What they verbalize about the service, they are more likely to remember and understand.

Remember, you are now worshiping through your ministry to your own child. As you guide young eyes across the page, listen to and answer questions, help to find a page, point out where we are in the bulletin, do not mistakenly feel that your own worship is interrupted. Welcome this opportunity to follow the leadership of the One whom we worship. Jesus said, "Whoever welcomes one such child in my name welcomes me (Mt.18:5)."

Format for Creating a Worship Service

Below are listed several items that may be included in your worship service. You may use any of them or add some of your own. Look at the order of worship that your home church uses and those of other churches. Use this format to write down ideas as you develop your service, then move the items about and set up the order of service in more permanent form, leaving out that which you won't use and adding items you planned. Here are a few points to note:

- The placement of additional hymns will depend on the subject and intent of the hymns.
- The Lord's Prayer may be a part of any prayer, depending on the intent.
- The children's message is placed at various points, depending on the church. If young children leave after the children's message, include them in as much of the service as possible.
- Note that some churches have the offering before the message, while some have it after it. When it is after the message, it becomes a part of our response to the message.

Entrance
Greeting/welcome
Announcements
Prelude
Lighting of candles
Call to worship
Hymn of praise
Ritual of Christian fellowship
Creed
Gloria Patri
Call to prayer with joys and concerns of the church
Pastoral prayer
Silent prayer of confession and forgiveness
Affirmation of forgiveness

Proclamation and Response
Anthem
Scripture
Message
Offering of gifts and service
Doxology

Thanksgiving and Communion
Prayer of thanksgiving and/or communion

Sending Forth
Hymn of invitation
Benediction
Congregational response

Young Reader's Bulletin

Our Church
Ourtown, USA
_____(date)_____

Before the service begins:

1. Say hello to people around you before the prelude begins.
2. As the music begins, listen quietly and get ready for worship.
3. Find the hymns in your hymnal and mark them.
4. Find the scripture in the pew Bible and mark the place.
5. Below, write the name of someone/something you want to pray about during Morning Prayer.

6. Find the asterisk (*) below so you know when to stand.
7. Smile to your parent(s) with love.
8. Ask God to help everyone worship.
9. Pray for the persons named below who lead you in worship.

Welcome & Announcements (Write or draw something mentioned that you want to remember this week.)

Prelude (This is when we prepare for worship. Listen to the music and remember God's love.)

Lighting Of Candles (The acolytes remind us that Christ is here by lighting candles.)

Call To Worship (We will read the words in dark print.)

Let us ask God to be with us and give God thanks.
Let us rejoice in our hearts as we sing praises to God.
We praise God who made the heavens and the earth.
We will sing praises to our God.
Let us always open ourselves to be with God.
Let us look for the strength that God gives us.
We know that God is with us in every way.
God will give us the strength to face each day.
Who can take God's love away from us?
Will hard times separate us from our God?
Nothing can keep us from God's love.
We will always have God near us if we only seek God.

*Hymn Of Praise
(We stand for the first hymn recognizing God, just as we would if a king came into the room.)

*Affirmation Of Faith/Creed (We say what we believe about God and Jesus.)

*Gloria Patri (We sing a very old song of praise.)
Glory be to the Father, and to the Son, and to the Holy Ghost. As it was in the beginning, is now, and ever shall be, World without end. Amen. Amen.

Morning Prayer
Moment of Silent Prayer (Remember someone you specially want to pray for. Write the name here _____.)

Meditation And Silent Confession
(Think of something you have done wrong that you want to change. Write or draw it here.)

Our Lord's Prayer
Our Father, who art in heaven, hallowed be thy name. Thy kingdom come, thy will be done on earth as it is in heaven. Give us this day our daily bread. And forgive us our trespasses, as we forgive those who trespass against us. And lead us not into temptation, but deliver us from evil. For thine is the kingdom, and the power, and the glory, forever. Amen.

*Ritual Of Christian Fellowship Or Passing The Peace
(We greet those around us. Think of someone you especially want to shake hands with today.)

Children's Choir (Your turn to lead the people in praising God.)

Children's Moment (Join the pastor in the front.)

Response To God's Giving
Offertory (We give God some of what God has given us. Do you have money to put in the offering plate today? As the music plays, write or draw an especially good thing that happened to you this week.)

*Doxology
Praise God from whom all blessings flow.
Praise him all creatures here below.
Praise him above ye heavenly hosts.
Praise Father, Son, and Holy Ghost. Amen.

Scripture Matthew 28:16-20
(Listen to and read the scripture. Write or draw something from
the scripture here.)

Ministry Of Music (Listen to the words of the song. Write or
draw something here that the words say to you.)

Message Title. . .
(Use this space to write or draw something about what the pastor
says. Take the bulletin home and talk with your parents about
it.)

*Hymn Of Invitation
(If you wish to go to the front to pray, you may do so now.)

*Benediction (The pastor sends us out into the world to live as God wants us to live.)

*Congregational Response
That's how it is with God's love
Once you've experienced it;
You spread God's love to everyone;
You want to pass it on.

Postlude As you leave, remember that God goes with you through the week.

Glossary

Altar/Communion Table: Table where the communion elements are placed.

Amen: A word that means "I agree," or "May it be so."

Baptism: Church sacrament or ordinance in which candidate is dedicated as a baby in some denominations and accepted into church membership in others through a ritual involving commitment to follow Jesus followed by sprinkling, pouring, or immersion, depending on the church's practice.

Benediction: A sending-forth, when we are challenged to take God to the world.

Chalice: A cup or goblet used for the drink in communion.

Chancel: Area at front of sanctuary where the altar or communion table is.

Communion: Sacrament of the Lord's supper or the eucharist.

Congregation: Members of a local church.

Corporate worship: Worship involving the whole church family.

Creed: Statement of beliefs.

Eucharist: Sacrament of communion or the Lord's supper.

Holy Spirit: One of the three ways we experience God, within us.

Liturgist: A person who reads part of the ritual during worship.

Liturgy: The work of the people in worship.

Lord's supper: Sacrament of communion or the eucharist.

Offering: In Christian context, gifts offered to God.

Narthex: Room outside entrance to sanctuary.

Paraments: Clothes used on the altar and pulpit.

Paschal candle: A large candle, a couple of inches thick and at least two feet tall. It is placed on a three- or four-foot candle stand. The lighting of the Paschal candle is always associated with Easter. It is lit at the beginning of the Easter service and each Sunday for the fifty days of the Easter Season or until Pentecost. It can symbolize the pillar of fire that witnesses God's help as the Hebrews fled from Egypt. From this we see it as a symbol of deliverance, and this symbol also holds true on Easter morning as we recognize the empty tomb and the great victory over death that Christ gave us. The size of it communicates a power larger than life itself. The Paschal candle is also lit for baptism and memorial services.

Paraments: Clothes, especially ceremonial robes, and wall hangings used on the altar and pulpit.

Passion: From the Latin word that means "to suffer," in reference to Christ's suffering and the time the church celebrates that suffering.

Prelude/Postlude: Music as we begin and close the worship service.

Pulpit: The stand for preaching and for reading from the Bible.

Sabbath: A day set aside for rest and worship of God.

Sacrament: A "holy moment."

Sanctuary: A holy and safe place, particularly the church building or worship center where the holy God meets us in worship.

Sermon: The message that the pastor brings from God.

Thee and thou: Pronouns used in Elizabethan times for "you."

Tithe: A tenth of one's income that is given to God.

Trespass: An old word for sin.

Trinity: Three ways we relate to God—as creator/parent, Jesus in human form, and Holy Spirit within us.

Worship: Giving God glory through many forms.

Study Guide

This study guide includes suggestions for each chapter. Whether you cover one or several chapters will depend on your time restraints and the suggestions that you plan to include in any study sessions. It is recommended that the participants in a study read the chapters before the sessions.

Chapter 1: What and Why Do We Worship?

- Ask members of the group to introduce themselves and mention a time when they have recognized an awe for God? What was the setting?
- Hand out bulletins from a previous Sunday. As a group, go through the order of worship and indicate the places that we might recognize that God is speaking to us and places where we might be speaking to God.
- Ask each person to think through a recent worship service and share with a neighbor a part of the service that was very meaningful to him or her.
- Say, "Think of that meaningful time in worship. How does it relate to your own personality? Was it more auditory? More visual? More kinesthetic? More contemplative?" Ask individuals to share this with the group.
- How, in addition to attending worship, have you celebrated the "Sabbath" in the past? After reading about the Sabbath in the book, how might your celebration of the day become more meaningful?

Chapter 2: Why Worship with Children?

- Ask the participants to share with a neighbor a time when they have observed a child in awe or in worship. It need not have been in a church setting.

- Reference the experience of Dick Murray that was cited in the chapter. Ask participants to share an experience in worship that they might remember from childhood. What made that experience a happy or an unhappy one?

- Move into the sanctuary of your church building. Ask persons to sit down in the pew at the eye level of a child. Ask them just what they see. Walk about the sanctuary looking for things that might be of interest to a child. Sit in the choir and get a feel for what the service might feel like from that position. Stand in the pulpit.

- Review and discuss appendix 1. You may make copies of this for the members.

- Discuss ways that your church can make a worship service more child friendly.

Chapter 3: What's in an Order of Worship?

- Hand out bulletins from a recent Sunday. Look at the parts of the order of worship that would come under the headings of:

  entrance
  proclamation and response
  thanksgiving and communion
  sending forth

  Discuss the background of these four parts of the service.

- Read Luke 24:13–35 and reference the chart on page 11 to the story.

- Go through your printed order of worship in the bulletin. Identify the terms that are explained on pages 12–14. Are there additional terms of worship that are not identified in the book? What is the meaning behind them?

- Discuss the various roles of worship leaders in your church. Ask several different worship leaders to briefly explain how they see their roles as prompters, helping us to worship God.

Chapter 4: What about the Sacraments?

Baptism

- At the top of a large sheet of paper or white board, list these headings for three columns:

  Water is life giving.
  Water cleanses us.
  Water gives us power.

  Ask the group members to list examples under each of these columns.

- Ask someone to read aloud one of the accounts of Jesus' baptism (Mt. 3:16; Mk. 1:10; Lk. 3:22).
- Discuss the different forms of baptism. How is each meaningful? Which does your church practice? Why?
- Offer opportunity for group members to share something about a special baptism they've seen or their own baptism.

Communion

- Discuss the names mentioned for this sacrament, giving group members opportunity to express what these names mean to them.
- Ask someone to read aloud one of the accounts of the last supper and the reference in Paul's letter. (Mt. 26:17–29; Mk. 14:12–25; Lk. 22:7–20; 1 Cor. 11:17–29)
- Discuss the difference in elements that various churches use. Ask group members to express which ones are most meaningful to them and why.

- Discuss the style of receiving communion that your church uses most often. Ask group members who have experienced different styles to share that with the group.
- Ask the participants to share some early understandings of baptism or communion and how those understandings have changed.

Chapter 5: What Are the Seasons and Symbols?

- Take a walk around your church building and sanctuary. Before you enter, note the shape of the building and any symbols or wordings on the outside. Stand in the narthex briefly and speak of how we can use this room as a transition into the spirit of worship. Offer a brief prayer, thanking God that you have a nice place to worship. As you go into the sanctuary itself, note the various symbols that are in the architecture and in the decoration and furnishings. Reference specific items to the information in this chapter.
- Ahead of time arrange purple (two pieces), white (two pieces), green (two pieces), black, and red pieces of fabric on a central table. Ask eight volunteers to take a fabric and hold it for a few moments, reflecting on the color. Then ask them to share with the class some of their feelings and thoughts about their particular color. Ask them to continue holding their fabrics and arrange themselves according to the cycle of the Christian seasons (purple, white, green, purple, black, white, red, green).
- Going through the seasons, discuss the colors and their meanings and the symbols for each. Ask for additional symbols that they might think of. Be sure that they understand the meaning of the "ordinary season."
- Speak of the additional special days mentioned in the chapter. Ask them to suggest other special days that your church celebrates.

Chapter 6: What's in a Hymnal?

- Provide hymnals for each person. Turn to a prayer hymn. Read the words together as an opening prayer.
- Select several hymns that have symbolism in them, and discuss the symbolism.
- Locate the Gloria Patri or the Doxology and sing it together. Recall that these old hymns connect us with our heritage.
- Explore the indexes in the back of the book. Take time to find several of the hymns in each category.
- Using a hymn from the "Index of Scripture," read first the scripture and then the hymn. Discuss how hymns help us understand scripture.
- Locate a creed or affirmation of faith that you use in your worship time. Look at the other creeds and talk about how they are alike or different.
- Select one of the scriptures on page 38, and look at the beliefs in the text.
- Read the scripture in what we call the Lord's Prayer. Discuss the meanings of the phrases in the prayer.
- Look at the other worship aids in your hymnal.
- Select a responsive reading or reading from the Psalter. Read it responsively as your closing.

Chapter 7: How Is a Liturgical Worship Service Designed?

Review the chapter as you design a worship service, using appendix 2.

Resources for Further Study

Baker, Brant D. *Welcoming Children: Experiential Children's Sermons.* Minneapolis: Augsburg, 1995.

Brown, Carolyn C. *Sharing the Easter Faith with Children.* Nashville: Abingdon Press, 2005.

——. *You Can Preach to the Kids Too!* Nashville: Abingdon Press, 1997.

Christie, Judy, and Mary Dark. *Awesome Altars: How to Transform the Worship Space* (with DVD). Nashville: Abingdon Press, 2005.

Dixon, Michael E. *Bread of Blessing, Cup of Hope: Prayers at the Communion Table.* St. Louis: Chalice Press, 1987.

Felton, Gayle Carlton. *By Water and the Spirit.* Nashville: Discipleship Resources, 1998.

Halverson, Delia. *Children's Activities for the Christian Year.* Nashville: Abingdon Press, 2004.

——. *The Gift of Hospitality.* St. Louis: Chalice Press, 1999.

——. *How Do Our Children Grow?* St. Louis: Chalice Press, 1999.

——. *Side by Side: Families Learning & Living Together.* Nashville: Abingdon Press, 2002.

——. *Teaching & Celebrating the Christian Seasons.* St. Louis: Chalice Press, 2002.

Hickman, Hoyt. *The Acolyte Book.* Nashville: Abingdon Press, 2003.

Miles, Ray. *Offering Meditations.* St. Louis: Chalice Press, 1997.

Moeller, Pamela Ann. *Exploring Worship Anew: Dreams and Visions.* St. Louis: Chalice Press, 1998.

Mor, Dean. *Christian Symbols Handbook.* Minneapolis: Augsburg, 1985.

Norton, Mary Jane Pierce. *Children Worship!* Nashville: Discipleship Resources, 1997.

Ritchie, James H., Jr. *Always in Rehearsal: The Practice of Worship and the Presence of Children.* Nashville: Discipleship Resources, 2005.

Stoner, Marcia. *Symbols of Faith: Teaching the Images of the Christian Faith.* Nashville: Abingdon Press, 2001.

Watkins, Keith, ed. *Baptism and Belonging.* St. Louis: Chalice Press, 1991.

White, James F. *Introduction to Christian Worship.* Nashville: Abingdon Press, 2000.

White, Susan. *Spirit of Worship: The Liturgical Tradition.* Maryknoll, N.Y.: Orbis, 1999.

Womack, Edwin. *Come Follow Me: A Study Book for Acolytes.* Lima, Ohio: CCS Publishing, 2004.

Index